Contents

Meet Katie, Jenny, Paul and Simon

Katie, Jenny and Paul are children, just like you. They live with their parents, and they go to school, have friends and enjoy doing many activities. Simon is older and he has just started work.

Katie is nine years old. Her hobby is an unusual one. She keeps different kinds of fish from all around the world. One day Katie hopes to go scuba diving to see the fish in the sea.

◁ Jenny loves animals. She has a dog, three cats, a rabbit and a hamster.

△ Katie has mild cerebral palsy and she can do most things her friends can do.

Jenny is eleven years old. She lives with her parents on a farm where she sometimes helps out with work. She loves the springtime when she can help to feed the baby lambs.

LIVING WITH
CEREBRAL
PALSY

Dr Paul Pimm

HODDER
Wayland

an imprint of Hodder Children's Books

Titles in the series

Living with Asthma

Living with Blindness

Living with Cerebral Palsy

Living with Deafness

Living with Diabetes

Living with Down's Syndrome

Living with Epilepsy

Living with Leukaemia

Editor: Carron Brown
Picture researcher: Gina Brown
Cover designer: Steve Wheele Design
Book designer: Peter Laws

First published in Great Britain in 1999 by Wayland Publishers Ltd

This edition published in 2002 by Hodder Wayland, an imprint of Hodder Children's Books
Hodder Children's Books, a division of Hodder Headline Limited, 338 Euston Road, London NW1 3BH

© Hodder Wayland 1999

British Library in Publication Data
Pimm, Paul
 Living with Cerebral Palsy
 1. Cerebral Palsy – Juvenile literature
 I. Title II. Cerebral Palsy
 362.4'3

ISBN 0 7502 4162 4

Printed and bound in Hong Kong

Martyn F. Chillmaid would like to thank Richard Aust, Head of Chadsgrove School,
Catshill, Bromsgrove and Cramar Cat Rescue, Birmingham. A special thank you to
Rebecca, Emma, Matthew and Matthew for their help in producing this book.
Angela Hampton would like to thank Ingfield Manor School, Five Oaks, Sussex.

Picture acknowledgements
Wayland Publishers Ltd would like to thank: Angela Hampton *cover* [inset], 10, 27, 29;
Tony Stone/Laurence Dutton 26, /Richard Shock 8; Science Photo Library/Alfred
Pasieka 11. All the other photographs were taken for Wayland by Martyn F. Chillmaid.

SCOPE has been consulted throughout the preparation of this book.

▷ Paul has joined his school swimming club. This is great because swimming is one of the best exercises he could do.

Paul is twelve years old. His favourite hobby is swimming. One of his arms and one leg do not work very well, but this does not stop him from enjoying himself with his friends.

▽ Simon always wanted to work with computers.

Simon is eighteen years old, and he's just started his first job since he left school. He worked very hard at his exams so that he would be able to get a good job. Simon has always loved computers. He began by playing computer games when he was younger, then he started to learn French on the computer. His new job involves a lot of work on computers.

Katie, Jenny, Paul and Simon are very different people. They all have cerebral palsy, but it affects them in different ways. This book will help you to understand what cerebral palsy is and how it affects people who have it.

The brain and cerebral palsy

Your brain is in charge of your body. It tells your body what to do and how to do it. For example, it tells you to breathe, it tells your heart to beat, and it tells your arms and legs to move. Many parts of the brain are involved in making a movement. When you want to kick a ball, the brain sends a message to your leg telling it what to do.

When someone has cerebral palsy, part of the brain is not working very well. Messages to the muscles that control movement are not sent properly or are jumbled up. This might make movements jerky, or muscles stiff. Or the person might stand or sit awkwardly.

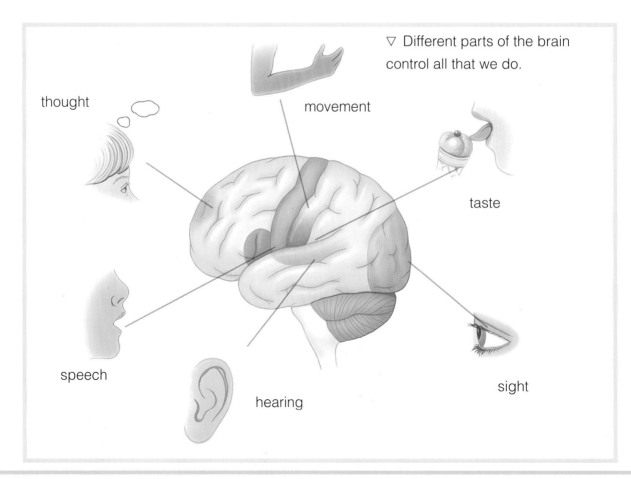

thought

movement

▽ Different parts of the brain control all that we do.

taste

speech

hearing

sight

Not everyone with cerebral palsy is affected in the same way. Some people are only affected in small ways and it may not be noticed. Others may have problems using their arms and legs. Talking or even chewing and swallowing may be difficult.

Sometimes the brain cannot easily work out what it sees, so people have problems understanding patterns and shapes. For some people, doing a jigsaw, tying a shoelace, judging distances or catching a ball might be difficult. For others, reading or doing sums may be hard. The rest of the brain may work perfectly well. Having cerebral palsy does not stop Katie, Jenny and Paul from having fun and joining in many activities. It did not stop Simon from getting a job.

▽ Paul likes to join in with activities at school. He was asked to act in a school play.

Why cerebral palsy happens

Cerebral palsy can happen in any family, in boys and girls, and in any country. It happens before birth, around the time of birth, or in early childhood, as a result of part of the brain not developing properly or getting damaged. Sometimes it is possible to find out why this happens. It might be because of bleeding or blocked blood vessels in the brain; problems during birth; or because the baby is born much too soon.

▽ This young baby is in an incubator. She would not live without the help of this machine. The doctor is checking her condition.

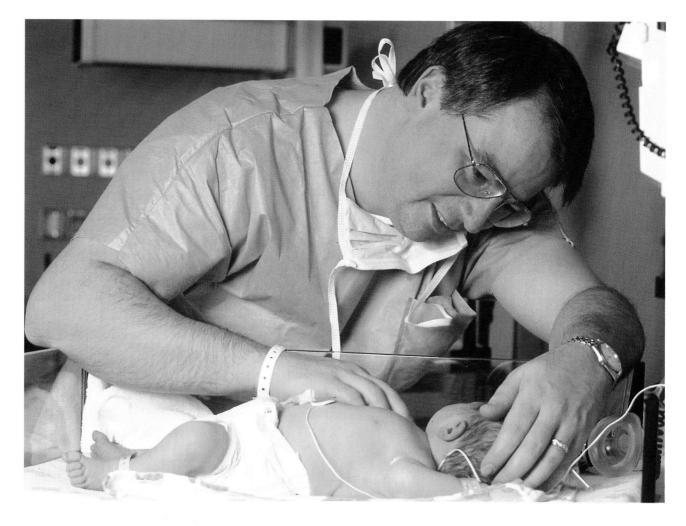

▷ Having cerebral palsy does not mean that your own children will have it.

Sometimes infections in the brain such as meningitis can cause cerebral palsy. It can be inherited, but this is very rare. Often, no one knows why someone has cerebral palsy.

It is often very difficult to find out why a person develops cerebral palsy. Simon's doctor could not be sure. This worried his mum and dad a lot when he was younger, but it did not matter to Simon. Simon's very happy with his life and his new job. Having cerebral palsy doesn't stop him doing what he wants to do.

Finding out about it

Sometimes the doctor knows that a baby is unwell before it is born. An ultrasound scan may be taken so that a doctor can see the baby inside his or her mother. This helps the doctor to check the health of the baby.

At other times doctors may not be sure of a baby's health until he or she is born. The baby's parents may be the first to notice that something is wrong because they spend most of their time with their child. They may notice that the baby is not feeding or moving properly. A person who is specially trained in problems that affect the brain, called a neurologist, may be asked to help. Doctors may watch a baby for a long time, and may take a scan of the baby's brain, before they find out what is wrong.

▽ An ultrasound scan helps the doctor to see how well the baby is developing.

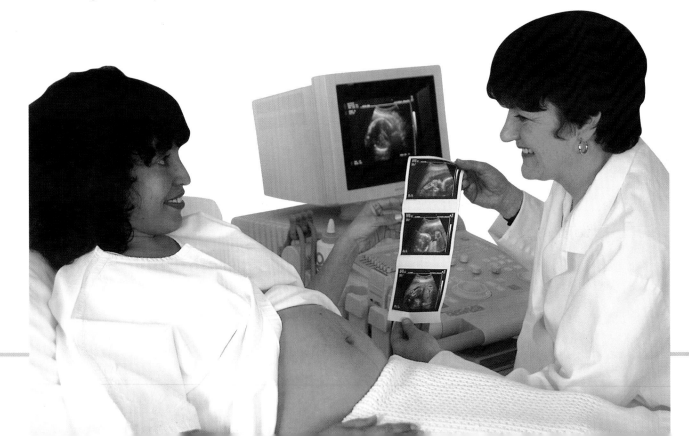

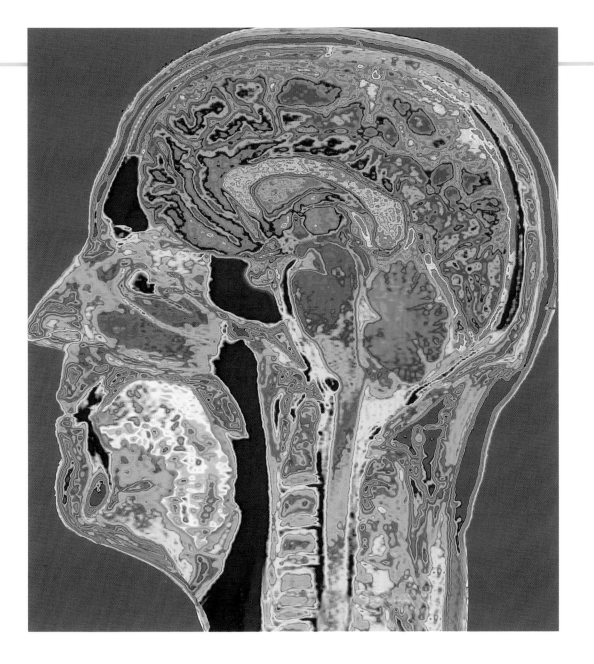

Some children with cerebral palsy may have learning difficulties. Others may have epilepsy. Some may have severe speech, sight or hearing problems. If the doctor thinks that a person has epilepsy, a special test called an EEG might be done. This does not hurt. Sticky pads with wires are attached to the head, to pick up messages sent out by the brain. The test helps the doctor to decide if a person has epilepsy. The doctor will then tell the person and his or her parents about the best way to treat the condition.

△ This picture of a healthy brain was produced by an MRI scan.

Treatment

There is no cure for cerebral palsy but, with the right treatment, life can be made much better. Physical exercises help many people to develop better movements, and may also ease stiffness. Sometimes an operation may be needed to help people move more easily, or to help ease pain or discomfort. Medicine may also help to relax the stiff muscles.

Jenny has a speech therapist because she has difficulty speaking. When Jenny first started her speaking exercises, she did not like them. Now Jenny feels more confident about talking and she feels a lot happier. She has a nickname of Chatterbox at school now.

△ Jenny's speech is getting better with the help of speech therapy.

Simon has difficulty walking. He uses a wheelchair a lot of the time, but his physiotherapist likes him to be on his feet for part of the day. This gives him some exercise, and it keeps the blood moving properly in his legs.

Paul has to take medicine every day to control his epilepsy and stop having seizures. Sometimes it can take a while to find the right medicine and the right amount to take. Paul used to feel tired and his school work suffered. His doctor changed the amount of medicine Paul was taking and soon he was fine again.

Katie walks quite well, but she may have an operation on her leg to make walking easier.

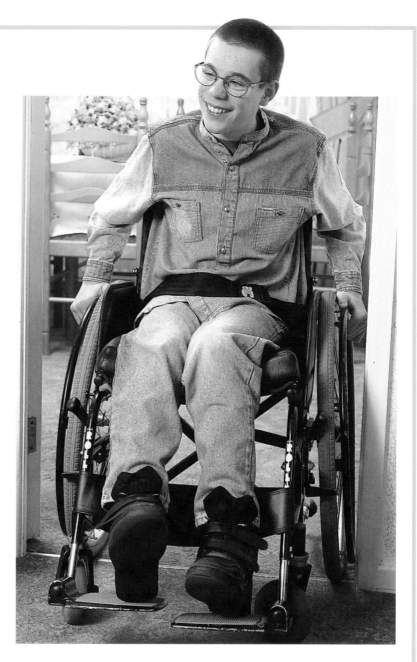

Some people with cerebral palsy have problems with their eyes. The most common problem is a squint which can be helped with glasses or an operation. Sometimes there might be a problem with hearing, and a hearing aid may help. Cerebral palsy doesn't get worse as you get older. However, someone with the condition can feel the effects of growing older earlier.

△ Before the doors were widened at his home, Simon could not get his wheelchair through the door very easily.

People who can help

There are many people whose jobs involve helping others with difficulties. When someone has cerebral palsy, he or she can receive help and advice so that life can be made better.

A child with cerebral palsy will usually be looked after by a doctor called a paediatrician, who is specially trained to treat the health problems of children. He or she will advise parents on the type of care needed for their child.

▽ The occupational therapist is showing Jenny the best way to use the special spoon, so she can eat without help.

Children with learning difficulties may need special help in school from an educational psychologist. Sometimes a child may have problems learning to read, or with drawing or maths. The child may be very clever, but needs extra time to learn some things. Educational psychologists visit schools and advise teachers on the best way they can help.

Cerebral palsy can mean that some people have problems doing everyday things, such as brushing teeth, bathing or getting around. For an older person with cerebral palsy, cooking and cleaning may be difficult. An occupational therapist can give advice on special equipment that will help.

▷ A physiotherapist is showing Simon how to stretch his legs. Some people need to do exercises throughout their life.

It can be hard to move properly when muscles do not work very well. With help from a physiotherapist, who can advise on exercises to do and how to move, movement can be made easier.

Some people have difficulty talking and their speech is not very clear. Others may have problems with sucking, swallowing and chewing, and may dribble. A speech and language therapist can help with all these problems.

Everyday life

Katie, Jenny, Paul and Simon are affected in different ways by their cerebral palsy, but some of the problems they face are the same. Parents like to protect their children, but sometimes they can overdo it, as Jenny discovered. Jenny is in a wheelchair and has some problems with speech. Her parents were afraid to let her go anywhere without them, but now they know that Jenny is sensible and will ask for help when she needs it.

▽ Sometimes parents need to be careful. Katie's parents need to watch over her, but she is allowed to play outside with her friends.

△ Simon likes to talk about his day with his parents in the evening.

When Simon was younger, he did not go out without his parents. Life got better when he got older. He would go out with his friends to the cinema or for a meal. Being in a wheelchair does not stop Simon having a life of his own, but he will always be grateful to his parents for their love and care. Simon has just passed his driving test so he can drive to work and visit his friends.

Paul has epilepsy and his mum was afraid to let him go out without her, in case he had a seizure. A specially trained epilepsy nurse explained how important it was that Paul joined in as much as possible. The nurse talked to his friends about Paul's condition and showed them how to help if he did have a seizure. Paul and his parents feel much happier now.

Katie at school

There may be some children at your school who have physical problems or difficulties with learning. Katie goes to an ordinary school. She has learning difficulties and needs extra time to learn most things. She has a special classroom helper to help with her lessons.

▽ Katie gets extra help so she can keep up with the rest of the class.

Katie has mild cerebral palsy so she can play most games and sports. There is a girl in a wheelchair in Katie's class. She doesn't have cerebral palsy. She was in an accident and damaged her legs. Katie gets on well with her but Katie gets on well with everyone. The teacher says it's because Katie is nosy and likes to know everything.

◁ Katie is a bit of a daredevil and will try anything.

I really like sports

'I like running. I fall over sometimes, but I don't hurt myself. I love swimming most of all. My physiotherapist says it is good for me, so I ask mum to take me every day in the holidays.'

When Katie first started school, some of the children teased her about the way she walked. Katie did not understand why they were doing this and she got very upset. One day she came home crying and it took her mum a long time to find out what was wrong. Katie's friend Sonia told Katie's mum, who then spoke to Katie's teacher about it. The teacher soon sorted it out and now anyone at the school who is being teased can get help. Some of the older children help the younger ones who are being teased by talking about it with them.

Paul at school

Paul went to a special school for people with physical and learning difficulties when he was very young. Paul liked it and made a lot of friends.

Paul's family moved house when he was a bit older, and he had a chance to go to an ordinary school. Paul went with his mum and dad to look at the school and they talked to the head teacher. Paul liked the school very much, even though it was bigger. His parents were not sure if he would cope with all the extra walking. However, Paul had made up his mind and his parents agreed.

△ Paul's mum and dad told his teacher about the tablets Paul takes to control the epilepsy. It is important that Paul takes the tablets every day. If he doesn't, the seizures will get worse.

When Paul joined his new school, his teacher asked a specially trained epilepsy nurse to give a talk to the class about Paul's epilepsy. Paul helped the nurse explain what it was like to the class. The nurse explained that Paul sometimes has siezures. His body goes stiff, his arms and legs go jerky, and he will fall to the floor. It only lasts about a minute. Sometimes Paul feels a bit sleepy and confused afterwards, and he might get a headache. Paul said it was not a problem because he could not remember much about it.

My new school

■■■■■

'I like this school. I'm not the only person here with a disability. I think it's a good idea for everyone to be together.'

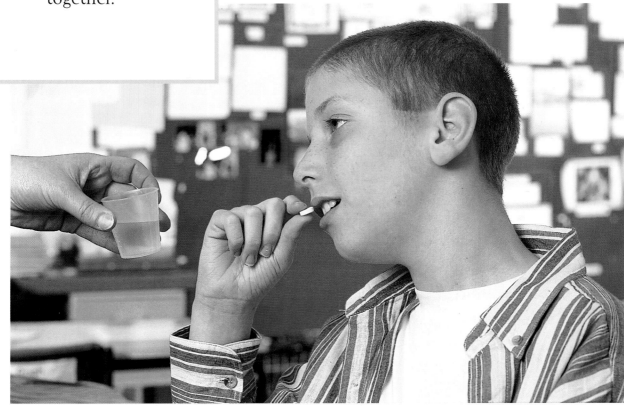

△ Paul knows how important it is to take his tablets.

Jenny at boarding school

Jenny is affected by cerebral palsy much more than Katie, Paul and Simon. Jenny goes to a boarding school. Her parents live in the country and it's quite a long way from her nearest school. Some children do not like the idea of going away to school, but Jenny quite liked it after she went on a visit. She stays there all the time, apart from school holidays and some weekends when her parents take her home.

△ Jenny's parents told the teacher how much Jenny is enjoying school now.

My first school trip

'I went on a school trip this year to France on the train. I need a bit of extra support, so the lady who helps me in class came as well.'

△ The electric wheelchair means that Jenny can move around very easily. But she gets uncomfortable if she sits in it all day.

Jenny likes the labrador dog that sits at the front door of the school and makes a fuss of everyone as they come in. It belongs to the head teacher. She also likes the swimming pool. She swims every day as part of her exercises.

Her parents like the school because Jenny can have daily physical exercises to improve her movement, and speech therapy most days that helps Jenny to speak more clearly. Jenny also has a lot of extra help in the classroom.

When Jenny started school, she was homesick for a while and came home most weekends. Jenny now stays the whole term because there are a lot of things to do with her friends at school.

Simon at work

While Simon was still at school he was able to try some work experience. The careers adviser found him a place in a big computer company. Simon was nervous at first, but everyone was very friendly. It was a large office with plenty of space, so Simon could use his wheelchair if he wanted to. He liked the experience so much that he decided to work on computers when he left school.

◁ Simon can drive to work now he's passed his driving test. Cars can be specially adapted for people's needs.

Simon did very well in his exams at school. He could have gone to college, but he wanted to work. He remembered the company where he did his work experience and he wrote to the manager to find out if there was any work available. The manager remembered Simon and, after an interview, he gave him a job.

In his first week, Simon put information into the computer and could not find it when it was needed. Simon thought he would lose his job. He did not, but he soon learned how important it was to do things properly. Now he is enjoying his job very much.

Exams at work

' I was surprised that I had to keep studying , even after I started work. I thought that exams had finished at school.'

▷ Simon worked hard at his exams and it helped him to get a job.

Looking forward

▽ It may take some children much longer to learn physical skills such as walking and crawling.

There is no cure for cerebral palsy but, with the right treatment and support from an early age, many children will go on to lead busy and happy lives. Some will go to college or university. Others may go to work after leaving school and some will have their own children. Some of the jobs that people with cerebral palsy do include working with computers, office work and social work.

For those with the most serious problems, support can be given to help them be as independent as possible. Someone in a wheelchair with very little movement in their hands would be able to drive their electric wheelchair. They could turn on the television, draw the curtains, open and close the door or programme their video. If they had no speech, they could use an electronic voice. All of this is possible with the use of computers. In the future, science will allow people to do even more for themselves.

▷ People with very little movement can lead their own lives. If they cannot do much for themselves, they can tell other people how to help them.

Katie, Jenny, Paul and Simon want people to understand a little about cerebral palsy. They do not want people to feel sorry for them, or to be embarrassed because they have cerebral palsy. Remember, people with cerebral palsy have the same needs as other people. They want to be loved, have fun, be supported and have the chance to learn about the world.

Getting help

If you, one of your friends or someone in your family has cerebral palsy there are several organizations you can contact. They will be able to give you advice and may be able to put you in touch with other people who have cerebral palsy.

Scope has been working in England and Wales for many years to improve life for people with cerebral palsy, and to help other people to understand what living with cerebral palsy is like. It produces helpful booklets, leaflets and videos. Scope has schools, a college, places for people to live, and centres where people can meet and learn new skills. It also runs an Advisory Assessment Service for children and adults, where help can be given on education and many other aspects of cerebral palsy. Scope is also a provider of Supported Work Placements.

Write to Scope at 6 Market Road, London N7 9PW, or ring the free helpline (0800 626216), fax (01908 691702) or e-mail (cphelpline@scope.org.uk) You can also contact Scope's website at (www.Scope.org.uk)

▽ Scope can give advice on education and schools.

In Scotland, contact Capability at 22 Corstphine Road, Edinburgh EH12 6HP. Tel: 0131 337 9876.

Hemi-help is an information service for children with hemiplegia. It provides newsletters, workshops, leaflets, information sheets and a video. It can also provide links to other families. Tel: 0208 672 3179.

The British Epilepsy Association (BEA) also produces helpful booklets, leaflets and videos. It has local branches in most parts of the UK. You can write to the BEA at Anstey House, 40 Hanover Square, Leeds, LS3 1BE, or you can ring the free helpline (0800 30 90 30). You can also contact the BEA's website (www.epilepsy.org.uk).

△ There are organizations that can help give advice on special equipment to suit special needs

Glossary

Brain An organ inside the head that controls everything that we do, by passing messages to the nerves.

EEG A test that records the messages sent out by the brain, to try to pick up any abnormal activity. EEG is short for electroencephalogram.

Epilepsy A condition caused by chemical disturbances in the brain, which cause seizures.

Hemiplegia A condition where one side of the body is paralysed.

Meningitis A serious disease that causes inflammation of the membranes covering the brain and spinal cord.

MRI scan A test that uses a very strong magnet to pick up signals from a person's brain, which are then fed into a computer so that a picture of the brain can be made. MRI is short for Magnetic Resonance Imaging.

Muscles Strong tissue composed of fibres which can get shorter and longer, and so produce movements of the body.

Neurologist A doctor specially trained to treat problems that affect the brain.

Occupational therapist A person who is specially trained to help people with movement and give advice on special equipment.

Paediatrician A doctor who is specially trained to treat health problems affecting children.

Physiotherapist A person who is specially trained to help people move more easily for example by showing them what exercises to do.

Seizure A problem caused when messages being sent to the brain get muddled up. There are several types of seizure.

Squint An eye that turns in a different way from the other eye.

Further information

Scope produces a number of leaflets and videos about cerebral palsy (see address on page 28)

Books

I'm Joshua and 'Yes I can' by Joan Bennet Whinston (Vantage Press, 1989)

I'm the Big Sister Now by Michelle Emmert (Albert Whitman & Co, Niles, Illinois 1987) This book can be ordered in the UK from any bookshop.

Living with Epilepsy by Patsy Westcott (Wayland, 1998)

The Illustrated Junior Encyclopaedia of Epilepsy edited by Richard Appleton (Roby Education Ltd, 1995)

For older readers

More About Ageing and Cerebral Palsy by Dr Paul Pimm. Available from Scope.

The Epilepsy Specialist Nurse Association has information packs for use in schools and by individuals. The address is: Epilepsy Specialist Nurse Association, Royal Liverpool Children's Hospital, Alder Hey, West Derby, Liverpool L12 2AP.

Index

Page numbers in **bold** refer to pictures as well as text.